POETRY

And

HOT CHOCOLATE

VANSH SHARMA

First published in Australia by Aurora House
www.aurorahouse.com.au

This edition published 2021
Copyright © Vansh Sharma 2021

Illustrator: Shradha Pant
Cover design: Donika Mishineva | www.artofdonika.com
Typesetting and e-book design: Amit Dey

The right of Vansh Sharma to be identified as Author of the Work has been asserted in accordance with the Copyright, Designs and Patents Act 1988.

ISBN number: 978-1-922403-97-1 (Hardback)

A catalogue record for this book is available from the National Library of Australia

Distributed by: Ingram Content: www.ingramcontent.com
Australia: phone +613 9765 4800 |
email lsiaustralia@ingramcontent.com
Milton Keynes UK: phone +44 (0)845 121 4567 |
email enquiries@ingramcontent.com
La Vergne, TN USA: phone +1 800 509 4156 |
email inquiry@lightningsource.com

*For my family, who motivated me to write more meaningful poems
and to create an eventful series*

PREFACE

I wrote this book in continuation to my previous poetry book *Life and a Glass of Milk*. I wrote most of the poems in this book during the winter season while sipping some hot chocolate, and thus, I christened the book as 'Poetry and Hot Chocolate'. While the subjects of my poems may be considered simple, I have defined them from the perspective of a young teenager.

ACKNOWLEDGEMENTS

I am most grateful to have the opportunity to publish another series of poems, thanks to the entire team of Aurora House.

I also want to extend my gratitude to my dear family: my mother who always encourages me to write more and to exceed my limits in everything, my father who provides for me and always makes sure I have a smile on my face, my grandma who cooks the most delectable food that fuels my imagination, and lastly, my grandpa who is always there to play with me or talk about whatever I choose and to tell me how to be the best person I can be.

CONTENTS

New York Pizza   1

A Stroll through English Fields   2

Cheerful Summer Time   3

The Night Time Is the Most Beautiful Thing   5

The Laborious Squirrel   7

Together the World Should Live in Unity   9

A Day on the Side of Bettington Road   10

A Poem on My Gorgeous Grandma   12

My Unique Grandpa   13

Regular Train Ride   14

Cheery Summer Time   15

Silenced by Others   16

Frigid Evening   17

Magical Afternoon   18

Light to Dark   19

Sunrise and the Purple Haze   21

A Town's Winter Morning   23

As Time Slowly Flies By   24

An Object's Possession   25

A Breezy Moment with Bears   27

Late Loving Autumn   28

The Kiss   29

Suffering Coastline   31

Picnic   32

Everything Was Completely Silent   33

Perspective of a Water Molecule   34

To Be Alright in Strife   36

Guilt Struck Heart   37

The Strange Lady at the Market   38

Special Reunions   42

A Group of College Friends Is Like a Family   45

The Lurking Mystic Clouds   46

A Child's Bliss of Life's Fortune   48

Mother's Love   49

Dawn of Spring   50

Mouth-Watering Tacos   51

Stroll through Sweetness   53

Anniversaries Are a Time of Celebration But Also Rest   54

My Sweet Cavoodle Puppy, Toffee   55

Lemon Tree Orchard   56

Humble Sparrow   59

Peace for the Worm   60

Longing of Bliss   61

The Striving Beehive   62

The Hungry Hamster and His Mad Master   65

My Sweet Kitten   66

My Lovely Puppy   67

Amateur to Professional   68

An Unsuspecting Biscuit   69

Kangaroo's Unwanted Delivery   71

Benny's Penny   73

Flowers in a Buzz   74

Fairy Floss in the sky   76

A Troop to the Park   78

An Interesting Escape   79

An Afternoon's Admiration   80

Grandpa's Serenity   81

A New Beginning   82

About the Author   85

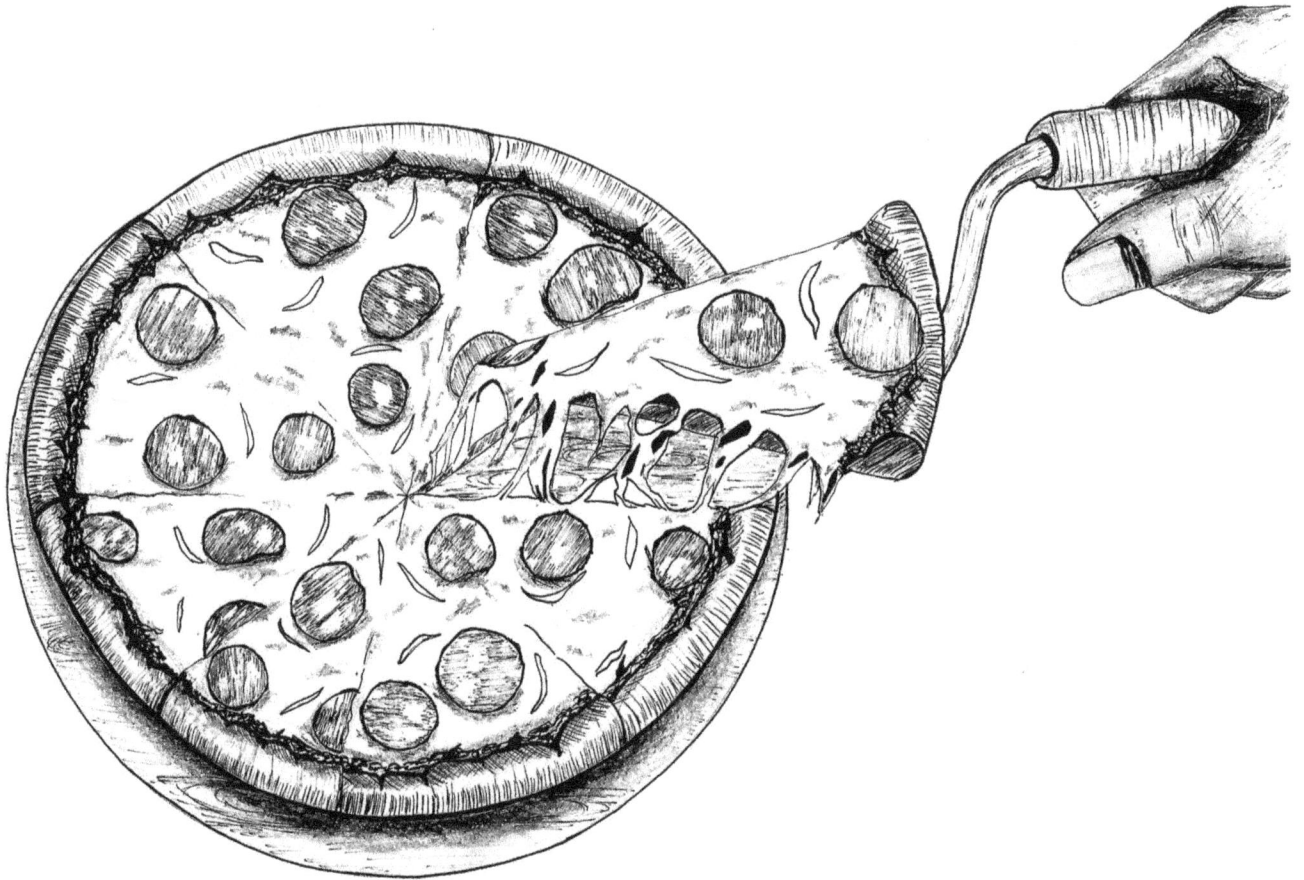

NEW YORK PIZZA

As I bit into my cheesy pizza I felt a rush of joy
The heavenly cheese stretched forever
A smile shone upon my face making me the happiest boy
As the deliciousness overwhelmed me; however

For me, a New York Pizza wasn't just a food
It was an opportunity, an experience to be devoured
Eating pizza would raise my mood and attitude
It transformed me into a hero from a coward

There was the perfect amount of sauce
And the crust tasted absolutely divine
I felt accomplished and like a boss
And it was like I was chilling on the coastline

With the beach and its waves by my side
Drinking a Fanta with my pizza
Thinking about my great sense of pride
Ah, there was nothing like the taste of pizza

A Stroll through English Fields

Strolling over the various pleasant pastures
I felt empowered... independent... free of disasters
It was nice to step out of a concealed aggressiveness and chains
And break out in jubilance from the awful penurious pains

CHEERFUL SUMMER TIME

A beautiful flower grows
Watching the sun rise
Waiting patiently
While watching the birds
Fluttering by to absorb
The day's first sunlight

THE NIGHT TIME IS
the MOST BEAUTIFUL THING

That mother nature brings to us
As it gives us the opportunity to reflect back on our actions
And think of the day's obstacles that have been overcome
But the most important thing is to rest
After the lights of daylight have been switched off
Of a whole hemisphere by mother nature
At night time I smile to myself
As I tuck into bed
And most important I thank dear God
For my great companions and family
Who make my night the more happier
And my day more blessed

THE LABORIOUS SQUIRREL

The squirrel hops through the grass
After leaving the tree for an early rise
Working hard like a student in class
Speeding to be the first for the prize

So he could feed his growing boys
And his wife who awaited him eagerly
Who would sit with an elegant poise
The nuts would save his family from living meagrely

TOGETHER THE WORLD SHOULD LIVE IN UNITY

By helping each other we'll have this divine affinity
We would succeed and be equal
To prevent diseases sequel after sequel

Arguments simply would not exist
If everyone lowered down their fist
Time would suddenly fly by
And only good memories would apply

The world would be at complete peace
Nations would unify from India to Greece
Warfare stability would be achieved
And corruption would be relieved

A Day on the Side of Bettington Road

I sat on the curb of the petrol station
Enjoying the view as if it were a vacation
Sitting here all day was but a mere temptation
As I felt free and without any agitation

I saw a gorgeous hummingbird flutter by
And some larger metallic birds in the sky
I always wondered how it would be to fly
But the fear of falling would make me cry

One... Two... Five... Ten cars sped down
And upon the drivers' faces laid a frown
It was as if they were racing to win a crown
I wondered why some were so angry and down

I stared across the large widened road
And saw a cute puppy so I bowed
On the owner's face, happiness was showed
I wondered how the puppy lived, episode after episode

I realised everyone had something to do
While I sat on my curb without a clue
Even the small puppy had something to chew
But I was as happy as a sloth in a zoo

I was sinking into the abyss of serenity slowly
Like a nacho chip stuck in guacamole
I was sinking but happily but unholy
I was eerily distressed but not lowly

I moved to the side of the petrol station
To watch the people of our nation
Fill up their tanks to roam God's creation
They were moving on without cunctation

I climbed up onto a large oak tree
And watched the termites smaller than a pea
Digging to the other side to be free
Even they had somewhere to be

Rainbow lorikeets chirped and sang
Eating the figs together like a gang
They suddenly rose up with a bang
And circled the trees like a skilled boomerang

A POEM ON MY GORGEOUS GRANDMA

If there's one person who always steals the show
It's my grandma, to whom I am obliged to bow
She's old as gold, but, God, she hasn't lost her glow
She may be short, but in wisdom she can only grow

Her cooking is the most fulfilling and utterly divine
Eating her food is my happy place, my cloud nine
Her kitchen and her food are for me to devour and dine
In cooking she really is the brightest to shine

Her aloo parathas are the only reason I can live
To me she is equivalent to the Hindu God Shiv
She never takes and only knows how to give
To make the best curries for her grandson, she is determinative

MY UNIQUE GRANDPA

My grandpa is the one whom I can go to
Whenever I have something very important to do
Or even if I'm bored and without a clue
He's always there to pull me through

I am the chip of him, he's the brick
In mowing lawns he's definitely the most slick
And as a doctor he never took a day off, a picnic
But when I'm away, he's the reason I get homesick

A man so wise, I can't imagine to be
All I can do is learn from his actions and see
So that I can become the best version of me
Foremostly, I want to be as happy as him and carefree

REGULAR TRAIN RIDE

I looked outside the stained graffitied glass
And listened to the rumbling and chugging of the train
I admired the thin smiling trees that stood near the grass
But the passengers had their phone glued to their brain

I felt as if they were missing out on the nature around them
The pitter patter of the rain, the sight of the rabbits
For their behaviour and unawareness, I must condemn
All I knew was that they were brought up with bad habits

CHEERY SUMMER TIME

---

before an autumn, love
under the flower

Silenced by Others

I was silenced from the crowd
And watched everyone
My cheers had been drowned
Long ago
But I still continued to strive
And make sure that my voice was heard

FRIGID EVENING

*A tall kangaroo bounces
at the perfect friend*

MAGICAL AFTERNOON

***

A compassionate boy plays
in spite of the wolf

LIGHT TO DARK

Light
exciting, innovative
smiling, achieving, cheering
happy, grin, darkness, sadness
stressing, stopping, dying
boring, frightful
Dark

SUNRISE AND THE PURPLE HAZE

I watched the sunrise and the purple haze
Creep over the barren but beautiful land
I recalled the old summer times in which I used to play
The orange circle lit up the land and encouraged
The purple and red sky to cherish
It was a beautiful sight that could not ever be forgotten
It glowed and brought out the smile of the early morning
And the indication that it was the start of a new day

A Town's Winter Morning

It was a cold winter day
With the townsmen feeling elated, I should say
The girls to the music would sway
While I smiled looking over the bay

The children threw snowballs and touched dew
And stared at the sky that was so blue
The spots of snow were a winter clue
So we rejoiced in the cold goo

And remembered the last winter time
That was full of hot drinks with ginger and lime
Coming back after skiing and scraping off grime
And thinking of a poem with a rhyme

As Time Slowly Flies By

The world grows wiser
But its beauty deteriorates
As the humans keep dominating
Day by day, the clouds and sky grow darker
Creating a barrier from the blue
The pollutants stretch the ozone hole
To let UV pass through
Further damaging
Our wrecked environment

An Object's Possession

Don't we all sometimes just stare into an object
And become possessed by a thought so perfect
It really hits you hard, last time I checked
If I am wrong please correct

In these moments I notice my mind is blank
If I'm being quite frank
I slowly sink into my thoughts and wonder why I sank
And then suddenly come to reality after the thoughts I drank

A Breezy Moment with Bears

The breeze whooshed through my hair
As I watched a territorial grizzly bear

It was so large, but warming in a way
That I cannot say

As it looked after its kids
Whom from danger forbids

And put a smile on passersby's faces
As it roamed the several places

LATE LOVING AUTUMN

A black, massive bear frightens
betrayed by the growl

THE KISS

Pay attention to the kiss,
The kiss is the most affectionate touching of all.
Does the kiss make you shiver?
Does it?

The deepest devotion is not passionless!
The deepest devotion is exceptionally fervent.
Disinterested, deep, deepest devotion.
Does the deepest devotion make you shiver?
Does it?

The feeling that's really warm,
Above all others, is the filial fondness.
Now fearful is just the thing
To get me wondering if the filial fondness is unhealthy.

A firm friendship, however hard it tries,
Will always be secure.
Now soft is just the thing
To get me wondering if the firm friendship is muddled.

One afternoon I said to myself,
"Why isn't the little lovey more wicked?
Are you upset by how sound it is?
Does it tear you apart to see the little lovey so effective?"

I cannot help but stop and look at the eternal, deepest dearest.
Does the deepest dearest make you shiver?
Does it?

SUFFERING COASTLINE

*A spiky scorpion stings
because of the sun*

PICNIC

Impromptu, brilliant
Stargazing, euchring, birdwatching
It put hunger at rest
Barbie

Everything Was Completely Silent

There was nothing at all violent
The lake was a clear pristine mirror
That slowly became clearer and clearer

The trees and branches showed no wind
And the very subtle breeze around me thinned
The leaves stopped their motion
And sounds ceased from the ocean

PERSPECTIVE OF A WATER MOLECULE

I free-fell down from the thick, heavy Cumulus cloud
And struck down into the large lake crowd
I was with my fellow freshwater molecules livin' the dream
I, after several years, had made it to Baikal – the best lake... the cream

I could now enjoy the view and the sea life for a little while
Before being sucked up by a nasty crocodile
Suddenly I got slowly evaporated as the sun had come out
And I became water vapour up in the sky where I couldn't shout

After a while, when my fellow molecules and I had condensed
We fell again, and on the side of a mountain I was slammed against
I was now a part of the surface runoff, which was like a roller coaster
I loved the ride until it came to an abrupt halt like an old toaster

I was soon soaked up by the soil of a neighbouring tree
I was now a major part of the photosynthesis cycle that I could glee
But I really wanted to rise up again to reach the clouds to escapade
I wanted to see what other water molecules dreamt, so I prayed

Suddenly, my gloomy mood lightened as I started to transpire up to heaven
This was a sign from God Himself; He wanted me to visit all the seas, the seven
I exclaimed in ebullience as I condensed after being water vapour and started to fall
I saw the grassy green ground. Plop! I fell into the mouth of an
ignorant teen bouncing a ball

This was now the definite end
There couldn't be a curve or another bend.

TO BE ALRIGHT IN STRIFE

In deep times of sickness and sadness
Try to steer away from absurd madness
And help those who are sick and in need
This is the only thing I plead

Keep striving and thriving to do what is right
And make sure that everyone is a bubble of bliss
Because all I can do for you is write
So that you can have something to reminisce

So do what you do best
And don't let the pain get to your chest

GUILT STRUCK HEART

A sense of guilt struck me in my heart
For I had lied to my mother
I knew she would find out; she was smart
At this point I wish I had a brother

So that she could spare me and take him instead
But I realised she wouldn't be mad
She would remind me in the head
Of why this lying crime was bad

Year after year I tried to stop
But the lies hung on to me
And dragged me until I would pop
And the lie would lurk like a flying bee

I thought I was a failure in my mum's eyes
An unfaithful boy whose love didn't exist
Except for the deceit and lies
Someone who was always full of twists

The Strange Lady at the Market

One day at a pet shop,
I met a man selling puppies,
For money he wanted to swap,
But I really wanted some guppies.

"Got any guppies?" asked I.
"For that's how I'll spend my money."
"No guppies here!" said the guy.
He seemed to find it quite funny.

"We've got some lovely bunnies,
I'll give you a very fine price."
"I'd rather have some sunnies."
The man blinked rapidly thrice.

The man seemed exceptionally mighty,
And his manner was strangely amused.
He wasn't what I would call whitey,
Great disdain he noticeably oozed.

Like others, he thought I was odd,
Some say I'm a bit tall.
Still he gave me a courteous nod,
As if he thought I was plenty cool.

So in search of my goal I departed,
But before the pet shop could I leave,
The man came running full-hearted,
"I can help you I believe."

"Puppies, guppies, you shall find.
Bunnies, sunnies, you can get.
You must now open your mind,
And get down to High St Market."

So to High St Market I decided to go,
In search of the guppies I craved.
The winds did eerily blow,
But I felt that the day could be saved.

There were stalls selling pies,
Cakes in many shades.
There were even stalls selling rice.
People were scattered from many trades.

I was greeted by a peculiar lady,
She seemed to be rather tall;
I couldn't help thinking she might be quite shady.
I wondered if she was at all cool.

Before I could open my mouth,
She shouted, "For you, I have some guppies!"
I headed towards her, to the south,
Past some bunnies and puppies.

"But how did you know?" I asked.
"Do you want them or not?" she did say.
Silently, the guppies she passed,
Then vanished before I could pay.

As I walked away I heard a crackle,
Or was it, perhaps, a hushed cackle?

SPECIAL REUNIONS

Reunions are a time of bliss
It is a time to spark memories with a family-like friend
It is an opportunity that you can never miss
A time to revisit the past and mend

Seeing an old friend after twenty-five years
Lights up faces and more importantly it produces smiles
It even shows up a couple of tears
And increases the memory that will last for miles

Sometimes you do not remember a bit of the past
Or recall a hilarious situation
But an old friend is there to make you think of it fast
And make you crack up in elation

Looking back at the rest of my mum and dad's 94 Batch
I see an array of proud determined faces
With different personalities like a vegetable patch
But somehow they have come together from different places

People in college batches resemble a large tree
They all come from separate areas like the roots
Then they come together to form the strong trunk
Later they branch out to prosper and grow their own fruits

To me a college reunion is the same as a family get-together
As the bonds that are created will forever last
And here you guys stand altogether
Wishing for a much longer and exciting past

But instead of weeping stand up tall
And discover what the future has to bring
But realise the people around you brought you to this stage since you were small
These are the people whom you should be worshipping

But today is a time to think and relax
And to converse in conversation about the past
It is a time to cut down the burning life's tension with an axe
So take a deep breath and go and have a blast!

A Group of College Friends
Is Like a Family

And a family is like a circle,
The connection never ends,
And even if at times it breaks,
In time it always mends.

Whenever we meet up with our friends
We feel a sense of joy in our hearts
We sometimes see how life without them would be an end
As there would not be a companion of arts
There would be no one with time to spend

But we are eternally grateful for them to start
As they encourage us to strive for the best
They are the furnace to melt our heart
And the piece of the puzzle to finish our life's crest
They are the coal and the steam to push me: the cart

THE LURKING MYSTIC CLOUDS

I heard the thick angel white cumulous clouds' cries
As they hung shallowly from the blue, moving skies
And moved like extra-terrestrial spaceships across
Waiting to hit the civilians with a rain attack or frost

After condensing the spaceship's bullets' fall
To cause the civilians to hide away into their cup
After the bullets' missions are done they call
The satanic sun to evaporate them back up

A Child's Bliss of Life's Fortune

Life is a joyful and miraculous phenomenon for a child
As they see the world full of creatures tame and wild
But they also learn how to be ordered and filed
And be independent, but listen when they have been dialled

But as they experience growth and mature slowly
The feeling of joyful jubilance can drop and become lowly
And entertaining parents can become stricter and worse
Unwanted decisions can be forced upon like a curse

Some may drink the cup of tar and others consume the pot o' honey
And the key to stay on top of the sea of unwanted desires is not money
Instead it's the inner peace and thankfulness to exist as a useful living thing
To steer from misery and dive to joy to become the ultimate universe's king!

Mother's Love

Mothers love is so warm and attentive
And their words are doubtfully incentive
They hold nothing but an embrace dearly
So we can hug them when downcast clearly
Not only are they love's source but they help
As time's advantage bulldozes we yelp
But the mothers diverge in, to protect
To importantly aid their children checked
My mum has the most enlightening smile
It lets me be calm and know that I'm fine
Most importantly, relieving me a while
Pushing me past the daunting finish line
Oh, the gratifying lovely mothers
Thanks to them dearly as they help others

DAWN OF SPRING

The sunlight perched over the tangled twigs twisted
And made the morning dew glint in the sunlight assisted
A new day's commencement had bangingly begun
And the hibernating animals emerged from the winter they'd won

The level of packed ice had melted to quench the thirst
Of the preserved shrubs and plants that could now burst
Summer had given its signal of an everlasting peace
That would always live on with the life of the forest and never cease.

Mouth-Watering Tacos

Crunch! I dived into my tomato and avocado-filled taco
My tongue, it swam through the pure handcrafted guaco
And my teeth collided with the hard shell of sun-dried corn
My body tingled and tangled with the new flavours it had worn
My body cheered in celebration of the new treat
And the taco tangled treacherously 'til it reached the stomach's street

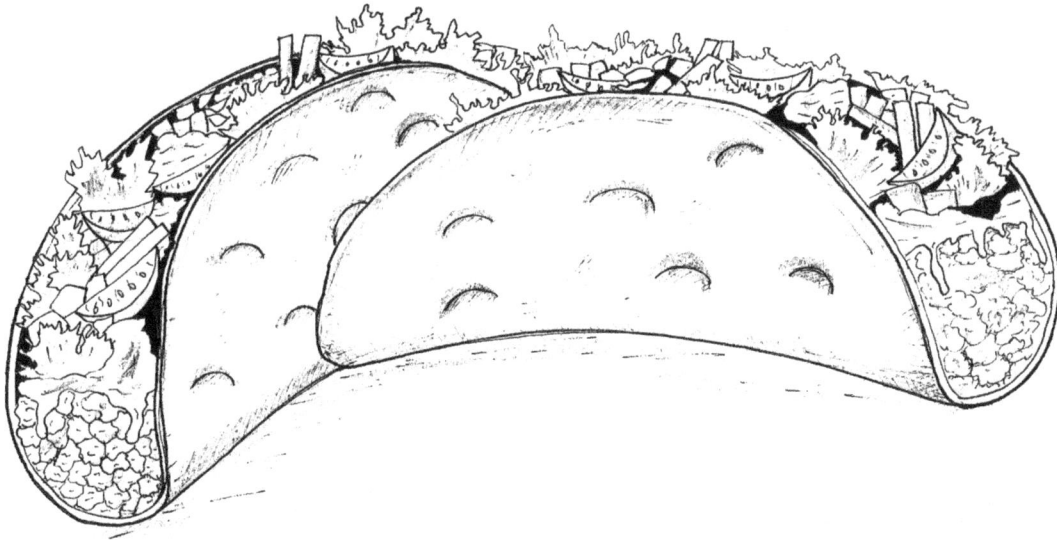

Stroll through Sweetness

I strolled by the acacia plants and the scent of papaya trees
The sun was tiptoeing down the edge of land, waving to the seas
And greeting the moon that came up as the sun went to rest elsewhere
And seeing the branches that blossomed with fire after they had been bare

I tasted the miniscule mingling mystifying marvellous mandarins steadily
And pondered how they grew out of microscopic seeds to make fruits readily
The citrous taste was sour but sweet like harmful thorns with an alluring rose
And it enabled me to recall a local gardener who'd spoken in polyphonic prose

Anyways, I headed back to my home deep in the urbanisation
To finally rest after a walk of strength that had caused my deflation

Anniversaries Are a Time of Celebration But Also Rest

———⚜———

Where the couples can reflect back on their life's best
And enjoy the fact that they have stayed long together
Even if they are opposite like a bowling ball and a feather

MY SWEET CAVOODLE PUPPY, TOFFEE

To my sweet cavoodle puppy, Toffee,
You brought love richer than coffee
And filled in the empty holes in my heart
To make any gloom sitting depart

You are the light to the dark
The love in all of the troubling hate
You give me that very needed spark
And open the happiness gate

LEMON TREE ORCHARD

By luscious lemon trees I went past strolling
Fingertips brushing the leaves consoling
Scent of freshness sour and sweet smelling
As the lemons protecting their emeralds compelling

I grabbed a lemon and whipped out my swiss knife
Cutting through the lemon's heart full of tension and strife
And squeezing gently to let a couple of juicy drops drip
Into my sweet mouth to make it tang on the trip

After I ventured through the smallish trees
That hung shallow hiding the bark
They swayed side to side by the ongoing cool breeze
One tree stood out though among all, like a matriarch

This lemon tree stood dominantly shimmering the light
And flashing its emeralds to appreciate the lemons
This tree had promising fruits allowing for a bite

Humble Sparrow

The sparrow flew through the mild breezes
And soared above the domesticated lands
It unleashed its mighty boisterous claws to come down
And lurch up a wriggling worm resting on the soft soil of earth
While channelling down the worm through its throat
The sparrow once again unshackled its wings to go and feed its children
Upon arrival at the sparrow's nest, a chick ambled recklessly to its mother
Who transferred the tasteful slimy treat down its throat
For its chick and nudged it back to the safety of the nest
This was a daily venture for the humble sparrow and its family

PEACE FOR THE WORM

Undisturbed dark soil
A thin, minute worm wriggles
Enjoying the cool

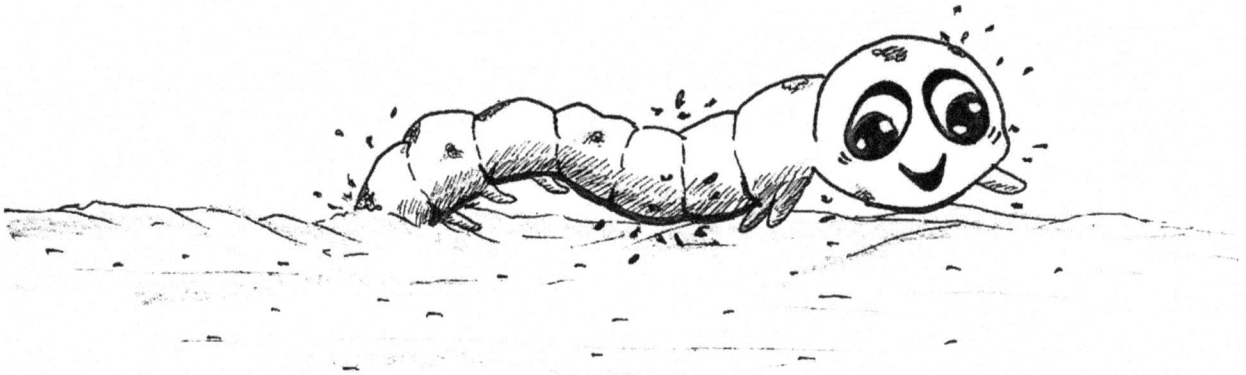

LONGING OF BLISS

The young prepubescent teen sat to recall
A time long ago where he had a time of best
A moment of bliss where the boy was having a ball
This pleasure moment of time he guessed
He had experienced with his friends at the mall
While munching on popcorn with a tang of lemon zest
And wearing his clothes for basketball
But he suddenly noticed while getting dressed
That true happiness didn't come from food or basketball
Rather from his friends whom he missed and blessed

THE STRIVING BEEHIVE

Once I was strolling through a path where one sees
A rather large hive with a collection of working bees
Buzzing off to their labour and pleasing their queen
And guarding themselves from the hornets unseen

The male bees ventured out to find undiscovered pollen
But on this perilous journey some soldiers lay behind, fallen
But others manoeuvred finely through the barriers
To extract the pollen from flowers to place into their carriers

Inside the hive the queen bee was busy inspecting
New baby bees who would have a job from the queen's directing
And work in the most intricate factory known to strive
Where labour was the main tradition: a beehive

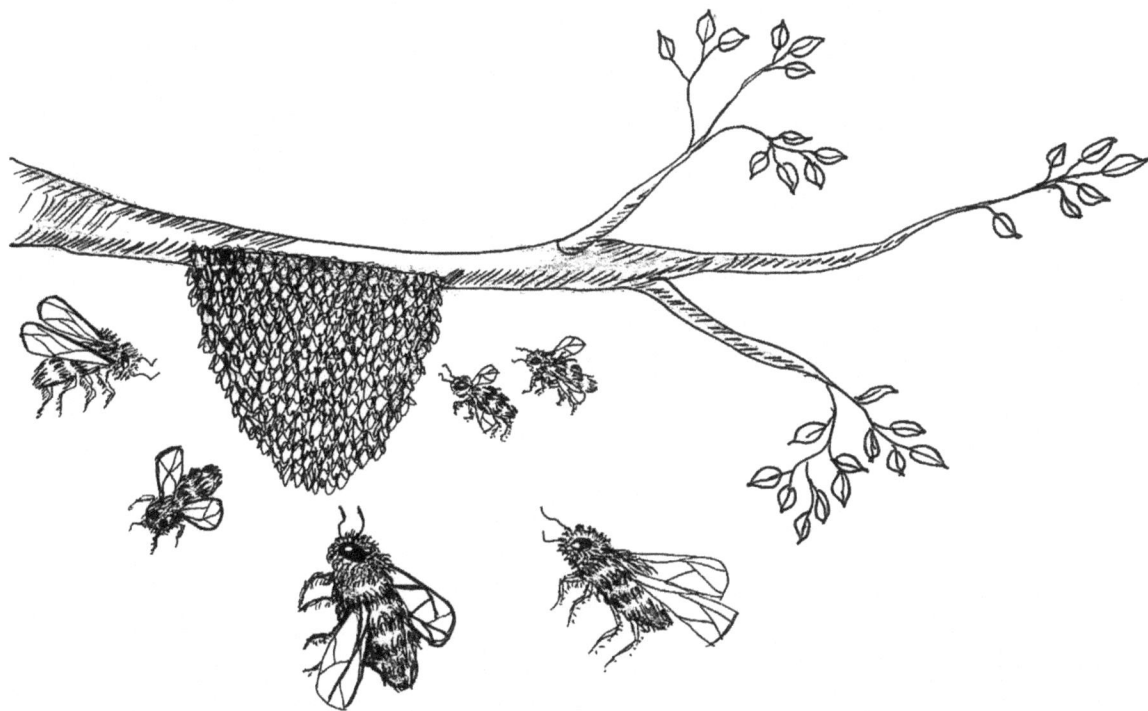

THE HUNGRY HAMSTER AND HIS MAD MASTER

Whose hamster is that? I think I know.
Its owner is quite angry though.
He was cross like a dark potato.
I watch him pace. I cry "hello."

He gives his hamster a shake,
And screams "I've made a bad mistake."
The only other sounds the break
Of distant waves and birds awake.

The hamster is energetic, hungry and deep,
But he has promises to keep.
Tormented with nightmares he never sleeps.
Revenge is a promise a man should keep.

He rises from his cursed bed,
With thoughts of violence in his head.
A flash of rage and he sees red.
Without a pause I turned and fled.

MY SWEET KITTEN

I love my kitten
She is so friendly and cute
She has a bold smile
And exciting attitude
She cuddles; I feel happy

MY LOVELY PUPPY

I love my puppy
He is gracious and clever
He has four soft paws
And a cute smile, furthermore
When he barks, I feel happy

Amateur to Professional

Amateur
Incompetent, sloppy
Lousing, learning, uninteresting
Weakness, inability, strength, expertise
Inspiring, interesting, striving
Dignified, executive
Professional

An Unsuspecting Biscuit

Arctic eventide
A giant biscuit rolls down
In spite of the barrier

Kangaroo's Unwanted Delivery

Forgiving sand dunes
A live, tall snake slithers
On the kangaroo

BENNY'S PENNY

There once was a guy named Benny
He said, "See my lovely penny!"

It was rather nice,
But not quite suffice,

He searched for more but there weren't any.

Flowers in a Buzz

How beautiful were the flowers on my morning run
They were at full blossom indicating their growth from the sun
And revealing their luscious petals that gripped on to the stems
That sparkled in the fluorescent sunlight like gems

Fairy Floss in the sky

The clouds seemed to float elegantly across the sky
Painting a beautiful picture in the air that lay so high
I also spotted children laying down on the soft green grass
Making out the faces of the clouds that slowly went to pass

A Troop to the Park

I trooped through the ever-stretching park
In which I came to every evening to see the lark
That would twitter and twitter
And gradually become quicker
I could see it aging though through the years
As it slowly backed away in the tree from its fears
It slept for hours too long in its nest
And one day stopped singing like the rest
Sometimes I thought that was the end of the lark's life
But occasionally it would let out a song of strife

An Interesting Escape

I saw a caterpillar slowly climb up my porch
This happened the other day while there was scorch
The slimy scribbling sloth-like insect left a trail of goo
As it casually swayed itself up the leaf which it was to chew
It suddenly saw my harmless attitude but was still scared
So it gathered up its leaves and wriggled away prepared
I was amazed at the agility and speed the caterpillar moved
It was in its zone as it crawled up the leaf smoothed
Finally it disappeared off into a distant bush where it resided
And there was the end of my happiness to be provided

AN AFTERNOON'S ADMIRATION

I sat on my verandah this fine afternoon
To recall my thoughts of the days soon
And for the abolishment of the day's sunshine
But for the dawn of the moon to be mine
I waited until the wolves howled and hunted
To warm up my hot chocolate after a day stunted

GRANDPA'S SERENITY

Pages of warmth and gratitude
Thought the grandpa as he patted his dog
He felt a true bond with his pet – one to last evermore
Fluttering finches flew fast through the trees
Which reflected the sun's mood onto the faces
The old man nodded with eyes closed at the sun
And remembered a time when he was a teen
Venturing through his own free world
And prancing and punching on opportunities
That made him the man he is today
Absorbing the new era's heat

A New Beginning

I hope this new year brings us fortune and prosperity
And gives us a break from all the trauma and drama in this world
Instead a smile for us to keep permanently on our shining faces
I wish for the abolishment of hate in people's hearts
And instead bonds to be made between the people
I hope God to forgive our sins by taking away this pandemic
That we call COVID-19 but others call a living hell
Unlike 2020 I hope this year people can go out and breathe with peace
I hope to see no protestors on the streets
While people go about on their daily chores
I hope they understand how blessed they are to live on this planet
May 2021 be the best year after violence, hatred and disease
Finally, may it bring peace and good health to us

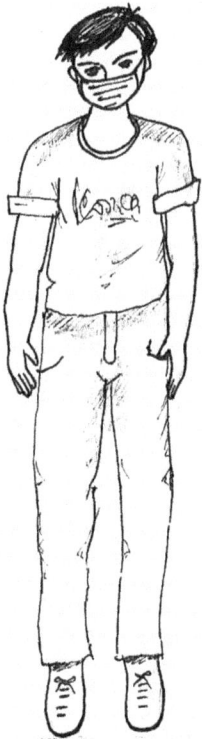

About the Author

Vansh Sharma is a published poet from Sydney, Australia, who is in year 9. He has a strong passion for writing poems about things from his day to day life and aspires to publish many more books that encapsulate aspects of nature and the environment. He is improving his writing skills and learning how to be the best author he can be. He is looking forward to future accomplishments and anthologies.

www.ingramcontent.com/pod-product-compliance
Lightning Source LLC
Chambersburg PA
CBHW040854100426
42813CB00015B/2797